Sally's Summer with Her Grandparents

by J. Matteson Claus

illustrated by Mark Weber

Scott Foresman
is an imprint of

PEARSON

Glenview, Illinois • Boston, Massachusetts • Chandler, Arizona
Upper Saddle River, New Jersey

Every effort has been made to secure permission and provide appropriate credit for photographic material. The publisher deeply regrets any omission and pledges to correct errors called to its attention in subsequent editions.

Unless otherwise acknowledged, all photographs are the property of Scott Foresman, a division of Pearson Education.

Illustrations by Mark Weber

Photograph 20 Getty Images

ISBN 13: 978-0-328-52667-3
ISBN 10:   0-328-52667-3

Copyright © by Pearson Education, Inc., or its affiliates. All rights reserved.
Printed in the United States of America. This publication is protected by copyright, and permission should be obtained from the publisher prior to any prohibited reproduction, storage in a retrieval system, or transmission in any form or by any means, electronic, mechanical, photocopying, recording, or likewise. For information regarding permissions, write to Pearson Curriculum Rights & Permissions, One Lake Street, Upper Saddle River, New Jersey 07458.

Pearson® is a trademark, in the U.S. and/or in other countries, of Pearson plc or its affiliates.

Scott Foresman® is a trademark, in the U.S. and/or in other countries, of Pearson Education, Inc., or its affiliates.

3 4 5 6 7 V0N4 17 16 15 14 13 12 11 10

TABLE OF CONTENTS

Chapter 1 4
Bad News

Chapter 2 6
Off to the Country

Chapter 3 10
Animals Galore

Chapter 4 13
A Job to Do

Chapter 5 17
Pet Adoption Day

Chapter 1
Bad News

Sally stood with her mouth hanging open, staring in disbelief at her mother. "You're not serious," she stammered. "You're joking, right?"

It was the first day of summer, and Sally had already begun to make plans with her friends. They e-mailed back and forth about visits to the mall and the movies and spending hours just hanging out. They had been dreaming of summer vacation since April.

And now *this*. All of Sally's plans came to a crashing halt when she went down to the kitchen for breakfast.

Sally's mother sighed as she wiped down the morning's dishes. "It's not the end of the world, you know. It's just a few weeks visiting your grandparents."

"A few weeks? *Weeks?*" Sally demanded.

"Well, a month," her mother admitted. "But you'll be surprised how quickly the time flies. You haven't been there to visit since you were little, and you loved it then."

Sally rolled her eyes. It wasn't that she didn't like her grandparents. It was just that they were so *old.* Of course they wouldn't want to do any of the stuff that Sally and her friends did. They lived out in the country and didn't even own a computer. She wouldn't even be able to e-mail her friends while she was gone. She would be totally cut off from her social life in the city.

"Sally," her mom said, "this assignment for work is a really big deal and I can't take you with me. I'm sorry you'll be away from your friends, but it won't be forever. It'll be an adventure!"

Before she knew it, Sally's "adventure" was under way. Sally had to admit she was excited to take her first trip on the bus unaccompanied by an adult. After all, she was twelve now. However, her grandparents would be waiting for her at the station. She sulked visibly as her mother waved to her from the bus platform.

Chapter 2
Off to the Country

The bus ride took her out of the city and into what seemed like endless fields and forests. When she finally reached her stop, Sally looked out the bus window and saw that, unlike the busy bus station at home, this was just a little platform with a few benches scattered about.

As she stepped off the bus, Sally's first thought was "green." The trees were green, the fields were green, even the benches were painted green. Sure there were green trees at home in the city, but nothing like this.

"Sally girl!" Grandpa swept her into a bear hug. "Look at how big you are!" Dangling as she was, Sally didn't feel very big.

"Oh, Fred, for Pete's sake, put her down. You're going to crush her." Grandma hugged Sally. "How are you, Sally? How was the bus ride? Are you hungry? Are you tired? Let me get a look at you!" her grandmother gushed.

"All right, Pat," said Grandpa. "I think Sally can answer your questions later. Right now let's just let her be."

Slightly dazed, Sally stepped back to look at her grandparents. She had to tip her head way back to get a good look at Grandpa. He was well over six feet tall. Grandma, on the other hand, looked like a miniature elf standing next to him. She was short, with rosy cheeks and twinkling eyes.

"Ready to go?" her grandparents asked in unison.

Pat, Fred, and Sally climbed into the station wagon and headed for home. As they rode along, Sally stared out the window. The town was so … small. Living in a city, Sally was accustomed to tall buildings, rows of stores, and restaurants on nearly every corner. And people. On a sunny summer day, there should have been people crowding the sidewalks.

Instead, she saw a sleepy town with a few shops and the occasional restaurant. The buildings were no taller than two stories. What few people she saw wandered along as if they had all the time in the world.

Soon they turned onto a tree-lined street and into her grandparents' driveway. Their yellow house had cheery white shutters and a fence around the yard.

"Here we are!" Grandma chirped. "Fred, you handle her bags while we gals go on up and check out her room."

As they opened the front door, something large and furry came bounding down the hall toward Sally. She squeaked and tried to jump out of the way.

"Oh dear, Boris!" Grandma said sternly. A huge dog skidded to a halt and sat in front of them, tail thumping enthusiastically. He panted as he looked at Sally with big, brown eyes.

"That thing is as big as a bear!" said Sally, wide-eyed.

Boris whined and tried to hide behind Grandma.

Grandma laughed. "Oh he's big all right. A big wimp, that's what he is. Isn't that right sweetie?" she asked the dog. He slurped his tongue across her hand.

Grandma turned to Sally. "He's a Saint Bernard, one of our rescued dogs. He's a bit shy, but he's very sweet. Boris, shake hands with Sally. Come on, shake hands!"

At Grandma's command, Boris held up his paw. Sally hesitated a moment and then took it. Boris pulled it back and ran down the hall.

Grandma laughed. "That's our Boris! Let's get you situated. Your room's upstairs."

"This was your mom's room," Grandma said, opening the door for Sally.

The walls were painted a pale lavender and the window had white curtains that billowed in the breeze. Even though her mother had moved out long ago, Sally could still sense her presence. Her mother's old toys and stuffed animals were arranged around the room and her posters were on the walls.

Grandpa came wheezing up the stairs with her suitcases and squeezed in behind them.

"Make yourself at home," Grandpa said, and they left her to unpack. Sally took a moment to look around.

At least the room is nice, she thought. *I remember staying in here before. Maybe this won't be so bad after all.*

Four hours later, Sally wondered if it were possible to die of boredom. She and her grandparents had eaten lunch and her grandparents had gone to run errands. Sally didn't join them, figuring she could amuse herself.

Grinding her teeth, Sally found nothing at all amusing about the situation. There was absolutely nothing to do. She was tired of her handheld video game, there was nothing good on TV, and she didn't know anyone to hang out with.

When her grandparents came home, they had dinner and spent the rest of the evening watching a nature program. Sally went to bed early. All year, she and her friends looked forward to their summer schedule when they were allowed to stay up late. Now staying up seemed pointless.

Chapter 3
Animals Galore

Sally woke up the next morning confused. In her groggy state, it took her a minute to remember that she was at her grandparents' house. When she tried to sit up, her head felt heavy. She couldn't figure out why. Then she realized that there was something sitting on her. She rolled over and looked for what had slid off her head. There on her pillow, a sleepy cat blinked at her. It yawned, hopped off the bed, and stalked away.

Now even more confused, she went down to breakfast. "I woke up with a cat on my head. What was that about?"

Grandpa grinned. "Probably should have warned you about the 'cat hat.' If it was the striped tabby that's Bert. The calico cat is Patches."

Grandma looked up from buttering her toast. "We meant to tell this to you yesterday. I guess you could say we're kind of like an animal rescue center. We volunteer at the local shelter and take in abandoned and mistreated animals. Then we help find them new, happy homes. Bert, Patches, and Boris were rescued animals that found their happy home here."

"Speaking of happy homes," said Grandpa, "we have to run to the animal shelter today. Would you like to come along, Sally?"

Sally decided to join them this time. She couldn't take another day of boredom. So she got dressed and they all drove to the shelter. Her grandparents sang old show tunes all the way. Sally rolled her eyes and sank down in her seat. Even though she didn't know anyone in town, she was embarrassed to be seen with the singing duo.

Fortunately, they stopped singing when they got to the shelter. Grandpa turned to look at Sally in the back seat. "Why don't you stay here and hold down the fort. We'll be back in a second."

So Sally guarded the station wagon while her grandparents went in. After a good fifteen minutes, Grandma and Grandpa came out lugging three large cardboard boxes with handles on top and holes in the sides. As they loaded them into the back of the car, one box began to howl. Sally jumped back.

"These are our new guests," said Grandpa.

Whatever was in the box hollered all the way home. When they parked in the driveway, Grandpa turned to Sally again.

Pointing to the box, he said, "Go ahead and grab the handle. I'd use both hands if I were you. Not only is Pumpkin loud, he's a big one."

Sally walked to the back of the car and grabbed Pumpkin's carrying case. Sure enough, it was heavy, and Pumpkin was wiggling. While Sally struggled to get Pumpkin inside, Grandma and Grandpa followed behind with carriers of their own.

"Into the den," Grandma called. They all trooped in and carefully set their carriers on the floor.

"Let's do this one-at-a-time," Grandma said. "Pumpkin can go first, since he's having such a rough day."

Sally watched as Grandpa unfastened the box and stepped back. A large orange cat sat up, stuck his head out of the box, and meowed at Sally. He climbed out of the box and walked around the room, continuing to meow at them. After a while, they sensed a decline in the volume of his meows.

Grandma smiled. "He's talking to you, Sally. OK, next!" she said as she opened the two other boxes.

"Puppies!" Sally cried.

Two puppies stuck their heads out of each carrier.

"These four little babies are going to be a handful," Grandma said. "They lost their mother, so we are going to have to pay extra attention to them." Grandma scooped a puppy up and it began licking her face.

"Woof," said Boris from the doorway. He sat looking uncertainly at all of the new guests in the den.

"Now, Boris," Grandpa walked over to pat his head. "Look how little they are. How could they be any trouble to a big guy like you?"

"He's afraid of puppies?" Sally asked.

"More shy than afraid," said Grandpa. "It's not just puppies, either."

"Birds, bunnies, cats," Grandma listed, "and thunderstorms."

"Don't forget vacuum cleaners," Grandpa added.

"And especially vacuum cleaners," said Grandma.

Chapter 4
A Job to Do

The next morning, Sally awoke and cautiously checked her head before sitting up. There was no cat hat today. She got dressed and opened the door to go downstairs for breakfast, but nearly tripped over Boris as she stepped out. He was lying right in front of her door.

"Hi, Boris," Sally said. Boris raised his head and panted.

"Good Boris. Give me your paw. Shake!" Boris lifted his paw and Sally took it. "Good boy!" she said, patting his head. "Let's go down for breakfast!"

Her grandparents were already at the breakfast table. They looked very tired.

"Are you guys all right?" Sally asked.

Stifling a yawn, her Grandma said, "Oh we're fine. Although, we might be getting too old to take on puppies. They had us up half the night with their antics."

Grandpa continued as Grandma yawned again. "We're actually thinking about letting one of the younger volunteers take them. With Pumpkin also being new here, we might have bitten off more than we can chew."

"Speaking of chewing," said Grandma, "did you see what they did to your running shoes?"

Grandpa sighed and shook his head. "I loved those shoes," he moaned.

Sally giggled under her breath. She lapsed into thought as she stirred her cereal. "Well, I could help out," she said.

Her grandparents exchanged a look. "It's a lot of work, Sally," said her grandmother. "Are you sure you want to spend your summer vacation working?"

"I don't mind, really," Sally said.

Her grandmother smiled. "Sure, we can try it."

"Excellent," said Grandpa. "With Sally's help, we could have everybody ready to get adopted on the next Pet Adoption Day!"

"What's that?" asked Sally.

"It's the day when the animal shelter puts all of their animals out for people to come and look at. They can choose the animal they want to adopt and fill out all the papers right then and there," said Grandma.

"It makes the process much easier," Grandpa chimed in.

"I'd love to help with that!" said Sally.

Sally found that helping with the animals was a lot more work than she had imagined, but the harder she worked, the better she felt. Her grandparents made it fun.

In the mornings, she took Boris for his walk. Every day he grew more and more playful around Sally. Her grandparents told her that she was good for Boris, but Sally felt that Boris might be good for *her*.

    Throughout the day, Sally and her grandparents spent time with each of the animals. They fed them and made sure they got their exercise by playing with them. Each animal had its own game it liked to play. Getting to know the different personalities of the animals was a challenge she enjoyed.

    Grandma explained to Sally, "Animals are very much like people. They have distinct personalities, and each has its own likes and dislikes. They have certain games they like to play and certain foods they like to eat. You just have to be patient and get to know them."

Then there were the puppies to think about. Sally's grandparents showed her how to feed and care for them properly.

"Puppies are a huge responsibility," Grandma began. "We'll have to keep them in their own area in the den. You can help us by laying down clean newspaper every day. The old towels will need to be changed regularly too."

"You'll also be able to help us by making sure the puppies get enough playtime. They need lots of exercise and attention," added Grandpa.

One day the puppies got out of their play area. Sally found them easily by following the trail of stuff knocked over, chewed on, or broken. Sure enough, at the end of the trail the puppies were in the hall closet busily attacking the coats and munching on another pair of Grandpa's shoes. Who would have thought that such cute little balls of fur could make such a mess?

During the next week, Sally's grandparents took her to the shelter to see the other rescued animals. The shelter took in animals of all shapes and sizes that were lost, abandoned, or hurt. If an animal needed a home, the shelter tried to provide one. They did an amazing job finding places for all the animals. Sally watched as her grandparents and the other volunteers played with the animals, walked them, and fed them.

Before long, Sally was walking and feeding the pets right alongside the volunteers. She also helped clean the cages. This was Sally's least favorite job, but she was proud to see the animals in a clean and dry home that she had helped provide. Most of all, Sally was struck by how much love and affection everyone provided the animals. Even though they would go on to permanent homes, the staff at the shelter tried to make sure the animals were happy and at home while they stayed there. What had started out as a boring chore was now becoming her best summer ever!

Chapter 5
Pet Adoption Day

That Saturday was Pet Adoption Day, when people would come to the shelter, look at all the animals at once, and then choose one to take home. Sally and her grandparents got up early to get the shelter ready. When they arrived, other volunteers were already setting up. Sally helped her grandparents take the puppies and Pumpkin out of their carriers and put them in cages. Then she paced nervously, waiting for people to arrive.

"Don't worry, Sally," her grandmother reassured her. "We don't give our little darlings to just anybody. People who want to adopt a pet have to fill out a questionnaire and pass inspection."

Soon people began showing up. Sally stood back and watched her grandparents work. Sure enough, they were very selective about who could take home the pets.

The puppies left first. Sally listened in amusement as her grandparents patiently explained to each new owner that puppies require a great deal of time and attention. To her surprise, Sally was truly excited to see the puppies going to good homes.

After a while, only Pumpkin was left. Sally walked over to his cage and reached in to scratch his head.

"Don't worry, Pumpkin. They always save the best for last." Pumpkin meowed in response and rubbed against her hand.

A little girl stood quietly next to Sally. Sally watched as Pumpkin and the girl stared at one another. "His name is Pumpkin," Sally said. "Do you want to say hi?"

"Hi, Pumpkin," the girl said shyly.

"Meow," said Pumpkin.

The little girl's whole face lit up. "He talked to me!"

Sally smiled back. "Yes he did. You know, animals are like people. They all have their own personalities and their own likes and dislikes. Pumpkin likes to talk."

"I hope he likes to talk to me," the little girl said.

"Meow," Pumpkin said in response and rubbed against the cage.

"He wants you to pet him," said Sally. She glanced over to her grandparents who were smiling at her. Next to them was the little girl's mother. Sally nodded her head in approval. Pumpkin had a home now too.

On the drive home, Sally was very quiet. She sat back in her seat, gazing out the window.

Grandma glanced at her through the rearview mirror. "Sally honey, are you okay?" she asked.

"Actually, I am," Sally said in surprise. "I feel like I should be sad. I miss Pumpkin and the puppies. It will be weird without them in their former house."

"But it's hard to be sad when they all went to such good homes," said Grandpa.

"Yeah," Sally said, smiling. "They went with such nice people and everyone seemed so happy to have a pet."

Grandma turned in her seat, "I can't imagine what we would have done without you this summer. Surely we would have had to give the puppies to someone else. What fun we would have missed! My favorite was that time when we caught Boris napping with the puppies."

Sally giggled. "Yeah, I liked playing with them. They were a lot of fun!"

"Easy for you to say," Grandpa said, trying to sound mad, but laughing instead. "My poor shoes!"

"Oh, hush," said her grandmother. "You know you had just as much fun as we did."

"But I lost three pairs!" Grandpa exclaimed.

Sally watched her grandparents teasing each other in the front seat. She wondered how they had ever seemed old or boring to her.

"Can I come back again next summer?" she blurted out from the back seat.

Both of her grandparents beamed at her from the front seat. "Absolutely," they said together.

Sally sat back, grinning. She couldn't wait to tell her friends about all the things she had learned from her grandparents. She wondered if there was a shelter near her home where she and her friends could volunteer.

How Can I Help Animals?

All kinds of animals need help. From common pets such as cats and dogs to more exotic animals like tigers and wolves, animals of all kinds can benefit from your aid.

Research

The first step is to learn about the animals that interest you. Several research tools are available to you, including:
- talking to animal experts
- going to the library to read about your animal
- surfing the Internet for more information.

Volunteer

Local animal shelters and humane societies can always use your help. Have an adult help you contact a local animal shelter and find out what kinds of volunteer services they need. Or, have an adult help you organize a fundraiser to benefit a local shelter.

Write a letter

Since animals can't speak for themselves, it's up to people to speak for them. Writing letters to your representative, senator, and even the President encourages them to pass laws that protect animals.